KU-484-612

JOHN HARRIES

Revised and expanded
by
Carola Hicks

Discovering
Stained Glass

SHIRE PUBLICATIONS LTD

Cover picture
Angel Minstrels designed *c.*1875 by Edward Burne-Jones and made
*c.*1910 by Morris & Co for the Birmingham Meeting House Chapel.
Now in the Stained Glass Museum, Ely Cathedral.

ACKNOWLEDGEMENTS

Acknowledgements for illustrations in this and previous editions
are as follows: Hallam Ashley 12, 13, 14, 22 and 39; Rachel
Beckett 1; Tim Buxbaum, 58; Jacqueline Fearn 47; George H.
Haines 17, 29 and 33; Martin Harrison 6, 7 and 49; Carola
Hicks 42, 45, 48, 50, 51, 52 and 61; David Ross 19; Jayne
Semple 15; Stained Glass Museum 9, 36, 46, 54 and cover;
Victoria and Albert Museum 16, 25, 27, 32, 35, 37 and 43. The
remainder are by Cadbury Lamb.

For the second edition of *Discovering Stained Glass* the
publishers acknowledged the help of Martin Harrison, at that
time curator of the Stained Glass Museum, Ely Cathedral. For
this third edition Dr Carola Hicks, also a former curator of the
Stained Glass Museum, has revised and expanded the text
further and advised upon illustrations. The publishers are in-
debted to her and also to the Stained Glass Museum for permission to reproduce several illustrations.

British Library Cataloguing in Publication Data. Harries, John.
Discovering stained glass. - 3rd ed. 1. Glass painting and staining 2.
Glass, Colored I. Title II. Hicks, Carola III. Stained glass 748.5'9
ISBN 0 7478 0205 X.

*Published in 1996 by Shire Publications Ltd, Cromwell House, Church
Street, Princes Risborough, Buckinghamshire HP27 9AA, UK.
Copyright © 1996 by Shire Publications. First edition 1968; reprinted
1970, 1972. Second edition 1980. Third edition 1996. Number 43 in the
Discovering series. ISBN 0 7478 0205 X.*
*All rights reserved. No part of this publication may be reproduced or
transmitted in any form or by any means, electronic or mechanical,
including photocopy, recording, or any information storage and
retrieval system, without permission in writing from the publishers.*
Printed in Great Britain by CIT Printing Services, Press Buildings,
Merlins Bridge, Haverfordwest, Dyfed SA61 1XF.

Contents

List of illustrations

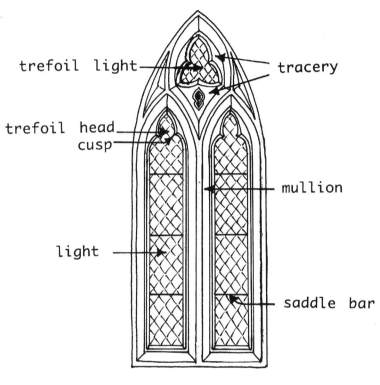

1. The parts of a window.

1
History of glass

There are stained glass windows in almost every church and cathedral in England, as well as in many other buildings, public and private. They have their origins in a time when the interior of a church was not tastefully unadorned but full of colour: pillars and arches were painted and walls were covered with murals; the woodwork of screens, doors and roofs was carved and gilded. It is not surprising that among all this were set windows of coloured glass. For whether pictures were painted on walls, on panels or on windows they were there for the fundamental purpose of teaching the people facts about their faith in a memorable and spiritually uplifting fashion.

Stained glass is part both of the architecture and of the decoration of a building. It is the only form of art which is observed through refracted and not reflected light, so its appearance can vary according to the time of day and season of the year; in sunshine it casts coloured light on to walls and floors. These magical qualities encouraged the widespread use of stained glass in great medieval churches, for light was seen as directly symbolising God, and coloured light as the equivalent of the jewels embellishing the Heavenly City of Jerusalem. Therefore, as well as keeping out the weather and providing a source of decoration and a Bible narrative for both the learned and the illiterate, stained glass windows physically represented Christian belief.

Glass had been manufactured since the third millennium BC before the Romans first used it for windows as well as for vessels and jewellery: they set small pieces of glass into pierced screens of wood or plaster. Fragments of such window glass have been excavated from Roman sites in Italy, France and Britain. However, it was more specifically the use of transparent glass coloured to create designs that was associated from the beginning with the arts of the Church. The earliest of such remains are pieces of glass painted with the figure of Christ which survive from the sixth-century church of San Vitale, Ravenna (Italy). In England, the earliest known Christian glass dates from c.680, when the Anglo-Saxon abbot Benedict Biscop sent to France for glaziers to work in his monasteries at Monkwearmouth and Jarrow. Excavations on these sites have revealed hundreds of fragments of coloured window glass, together with the lead strips which held them in place. There is, however, no evidence of painting to create a figural design, and the glass may simply have been arranged as a coloured mosaic. Elsewhere have been found fragments of eighth- to tenth-century glass from England and from Europe. At least one Anglo-Saxon monastery, at Glastonbury, had a glass work-shop, where remains of furnaces, coloured glass and lead have been found.

Written evidence confirms the existence of coloured and decorated windows in churches and monasteries before the twelfth century; there are early painted heads from the abbeys of Lorsch and Wissembourg, Germany, dating from the eleventh century. The earliest windows still in position in a building are the 'Prophet' windows in Augsburg Cathedral, which date from around 1100, but whose confident and mature style suggests the culmination of a long tradition. Further evidence of such a tradition comes from the twelfth-century manual *On Diverse Arts* written by a German monk, Theophilus, who describes the complex and clearly well established technique of making a stained glass window by processes which remain substantially the same today.

One of the influences must have been that of metalworking, because the production of enamel jewellery involves setting pieces of enamel glass in frames of metal strips, which also form the outline of the pattern. This is exactly the way in which pieces of coloured glass are surrounded by the lead strips which contribute to the design. France was a centre both of glass production and of enamel working, and it was probably here that the different techniques were combined in the early Middle Ages.

Stained glass became an important part of the Romanesque and earliest Gothic architecture of the twelfth century. In France, windows survive in the cathedrals of Chartres, St Denis and Le Mans; in England the most significant windows are in Canterbury Cathedral and date from the late twelfth century when French architects and glaziers were employed on the rebuilding of the choir and Trinity Chapel, the first Gothic structure in England. Stained glass was an even more integral element of later Gothic buildings, since the new structural techniques enabled much of the wall surface to be replaced by windows. The great walls of glass became tapestries of light and colour which, through their subject matter, also formed a part of the teaching of the church.

2. Canterbury Cathedral: Trinity Chapel, window XII, *c*.1200. Pilgrims and William of Gloucester. After Thomas à Becket was martyred in 1170, his shrine became a focus for pilgrims because of the miraculous cures that took place there.

Romanesque

Gothic
Early English

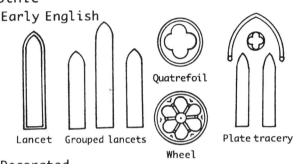

Lancet   Grouped lancets

Quatrefoil

Wheel

Plate tracery

Decorated

 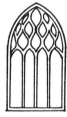 

Geometrical   Reticulated   Curvilinear

Perpendicular

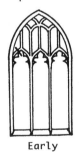 

Early   Late   Late

3. The development of window style, *c.*1066-1540

From the thirteenth century to the fifteenth, stained glass windows changed to complement successive architectural styles, with increasing emphasis on elongated figures (because window openings became longer and narrower) and on lighter colour tones to match the soaring buildings. The humanism of the Renaissance from the late fifteenth century, with its new pictorialism and realism, brought marked changes of style and led to a period of decline; the mysterious and spiritually uplifting effects of light streaming through coloured glass were no longer deemed so relevant a part of religious worship. In addition, creating realistic pictures undermined the essentially two-dimensional nature of glass design, while the introduction of coloured enamel paints meant that it was no longer necessary to have separate pieces of coloured glass.

This meant that rectangular panels could often be used and therefore windows became the equivalent of a painter's canvas. Unfortunately, unlike coloured pot-metal glass, which transmits light, paint on the surface of glass excludes it; painted windows made interiors darker, thereby helping to bring about further decline in their popularity. The traditional delineating role of the leads was also lost.

External and political factors also caused major changes in style and affected the survival of existing windows. During the religious upheavals of the sixteenth century, it was believed that the subject matter of much stained glass represented the power and rituals of the Catholic church, and it was therefore deemed inappropriate in the Protestant churches of northern Europe. In England, after Henry VIII dissolved the monasteries in 1536-40, not only were many great buildings with fine windows pulled down, but the main sources of patronage for future work and for repairs were lost. The process continued under Edward VI, when a Royal Injunction of 1547 decreed that 'they shall take away ... all other monuments of feigned miracles, pilgrimages, idolatry and superstition; so that there remain no memory of the same in walls, glass-windows or elsewhere in their churches or houses'.

Many churches followed these instructions and, where the glass was not simply smashed or removed for reuse, replaced their stained glass with clear windows. At St Michael-at-Plea it was planned to spend £20 on 'the new glassing of xvij windows wherin were contained the lyves of certen prophane histories, and other olde wyndows in our church'. At St Lawrence's

4. Holy Trinity, Long Melford, Suffolk. Large fifteenth-century donor figures of the Clopton family.

church in Reading the operation cost £15. Carrying out the injunction could be an expensive business – it was cheaper not to replace the windows but simply to knock them out. At Long Melford, Suffolk, 'Fyrmyer the Glasyer of Sudbury' was paid 11 shillings 'for defacing of the sentences and imagerie in the glass windowes'.

This extreme policy had to be reversed and a year after the accession of Elizabeth I the Royal Injunctions of 1559 added to that of 1547 'preserving nevertheless or repairing the walls and glass windows'. Stained glass windows were elevated to the status of 'Monuments of Antiquity', especially if commemorating a donor and it became an offence punishable by imprisonment to 'breake downe or deface any image in glasse-windows in any Church without consent of the Ordinary'. But reprieving windows did not reverse the effects of the earlier condemnation; many were still broken or left to decay, further depressing a flagging industry. In his *Description of England*, published in 1577, William Harrison, rector of Radwinter in Essex, writes:

5. Holy Trinity, Long Melford, Suffolk. Three fifteenth-century donors: Sir William Howard, Chief Justice of England; Richard Pigot, judge; John Haugh, judge.

'As for the churches themselves, belles and times of morning & evening praier remain as in times past, saving that all images. shrines, tabernacles, rood loftes & monuments of idolatrie are removed, taken down & defaced: Onlie the stories in glass windows excepted, which, for want of sufficient store of new stuffe, & by reason of extreme charge that should grow by the alteration of the same into white panes throughout the realm, are not altogether abolished in most places at once, but by little and little suffered to decaie that white glass may be set up in their roomes.'

There was a brief revival of religious pictorial glass painting in the reign of Charles I, but this was rapidly succeeded by further destruction under Oliver Cromwell and the Commonwealth. 'Superstitious pictures, images, ornaments and relics of idolatry' were anathema to Cromwell, and their destruction was ordered by the House of Commons in 1643, when there began the greatest deliberate onslaught on stained glass in its history. The fanatical William Dowsing, who held the office of

Parliamentary Visitor, gives details in his diary of a journey through parts of East Anglia, undertaken for the express purpose of stripping the churches of ornament and smashing the stained glass 'like a Bedlam', while the windows of several great cathedrals were destroyed by Cromwell's soldiers: 'Lord, what a work was here! What clattering of glasses! What beating down of walls! What tearing up of monuments!' Stained glass was associated with 'damnable pride' and 'the father of Darkness'. Richard Culmer, the rector of Chartham in Kent, known as 'Blue Dick', broke as much glass as possible at Canterbury Cathedral. He came to the Royal window and climbed to 'the top of the citie ladder, near 60 steps high, with a whole pike in his hand ratling down proud Becket's glassy bones'. It was quite common at this time to remove or break only the heads of figures – even of the dragons in the tracery lights in one instance. Sometimes faces were merely scratched across. But extensive as this destruction was, contemporary accounts make it clear that a great deal of glass remained, though often in a state of poor repair.

The objection was to religious pictures and not to stained glass, so while in the Catholic countries of Europe religious pictorial windows continued to be produced in the sixteenth and seventeenth centuries, in England glaziers had to turn to secular subjects such as heraldry, animals and floral designs.

The religious wars in France in the seventeenth century dealt the craft another blow when in 1633 Louis XIII destroyed the town of Lorraine and with it the glass workshops, the main source of pot-metal (coloured glass) for much of Europe.

Throughout the eighteenth century stained glass was thought of in terms of a translucent oil painting and lead was rarely used to outline the design. Then, after two centuries of decline, there was a great revival in England in the nineteenth century, beginning with the Church Building Act of 1818 to build new churches in areas previously unprovided for (under which six hundred new churches were built) and blossoming with the Victorians as they built new churches and restored old ones in a deliberately medieval style as part of the Gothic Revival move-

6. (Opposite page) St Alkmund, Shrewsbury. The Assumption of the Virgin (after Guido Reni) by Francis Eginton, 1795. The window is treated like an oil painting.

ment. In an age of urban growth and industrialisation, it was believed that it was possible, as well as necessary, to rediscover the devout Christianity ascribed to the Middle Ages, and that this could be achieved through the direct imitation of the physical surroundings.

The surviving products of medieval craftsmen were faithfully restored and copied; stained glass was recognised as a vital part of this process, for as well as being an architectural feature it expressed medieval beliefs. Thus it was initially through restoration that the long-forgotten methods of medieval glazing were revived.

Nineteenth-century glass is therefore basically modelled on earlier styles, in much of Europe as well as in Britain. It was not until the early twentieth century that abstract designs in glass became acceptable, with Germany and the United States of America leading the field; such windows are in any case more appropriate for the modern buildings for which they were designed. But the representational tradition is still popular today and many recent windows in churches show the biblical images which can be traced back to the Middle Ages. However, the majority of surviving windows in England are Victorian and deserve to be studied in their own right, as well as in relation to the fine medieval work which inspired them.

7. All Saints, Misterton, Nottinghamshire. The Five Wounds by John Piper, 1966.

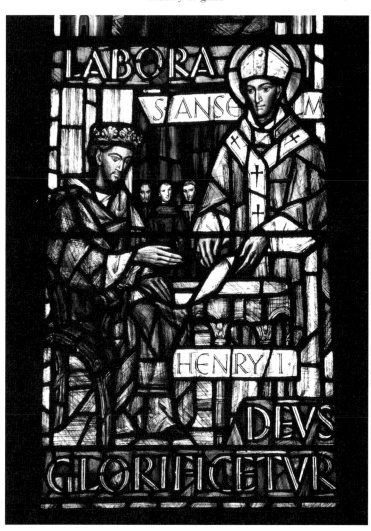

8. Norwich Cathedral. A scene from the Benedictines window by Moira Forsyth, 1964, showing detailed figure drawing and integral lettering.

2
The techniques of stained glass

How glass is made

Although modern equipment and mass-production techniques have streamlined the processes of the past, the basic ingredients and many of the methods have hardly changed from the Middle Ages. Transparent, or 'white', glass is made from sand, soda or lime, and potash (the two last ingredients acting as flux to assist the melting process), heated together in a furnace until the ingredients fuse to form liquid glass.

Coloured glass is produced by adding various metal oxides to the mixture before melting and is known as *pot-metal*. Copper oxide produces red, or 'ruby'; manganese oxide produces purple; iron oxide produces various greens or a bright yellow, according to the amount and temperature. Impurities in these oxides can lead to a very wide range of colours.

There were originally two ways of turning the soft, heated mass of glass into the sheets required for windows. In the *cylinder* or *muff* process, a lump of molten glass was collected on the end of the blowpipe and blown to a balloon shape. At the same time it was swung to and fro by the glassmaker so that the balloon became elongated. This was a slow process and the glass might have to be reheated at the 'glory hole' or opening of the furnace. When the balloon was the right size and length it was detached from the blowpipe and opened up at both ends with a caliper-like tool. It was then cylindrical in shape and looked like a muff. This was split along its length with a hot iron and heated to soften it again. It remained then only to flatten it out with a wooden tool. Sheets so formed were probably small, about 12 by 10 inches (25 by 31 cm), and were called *tables*.

In the *crown* process the glass was blown and rolled into a round bubble, the nub of which was picked up by an iron rod; then the blowpipe was cut off, leaving an opening. The rod was spun rapidly while the opening was gradually enlarged with the caliper tool and the ball of glass eventually became a circular sheet, or crown. When this was completely flat it was broken off the rod. A crown was between 12 and 24 inches (25 and 50 cm) in diameter and thickest in the centre where the rod was attached the crown or bull's eye, which could be used for decorative effects.

Sheets of glass were annealed for one to four days. It can be seen, therefore, that making enough glass for a large window would require a great deal of time, care and patience. Whether crown or muff glass has been used in a window can be determined from the direction of the minute air bubbles in the glass; in muff glass, they form straight, parallel lines, while in crown glass they form widening concentric circles.

A more recent type of glass is *Norman slab*, made by blowing the molten mixture into a box-shaped mould, which then produces five rectangular sheets; these are deliberately thick-textured, creating more interesting effects. The process was invented in 1889 to the commission of the architect Edward Prior, who was dissatisfied with the existing quality of glass for the windows in his churches. A twentieth-century refinement of this is *dalle de verre*, extremely thick slabs which are cast by pouring molten glass into a mould.

All glass blown by mouth is called *antique* glass; it is still being produced but, as a hand-made product, is the most expensive. Commercial or *cathedral* glass is machine-made by rollers. The most recent mass-production technique is that of *float-glass*, made on a layer of molten tin.

There is another kind of coloured glass called *flash* glass, which is made by coating or flashing white glass with a thin layer of coloured glass at the molten stage: flash glass was thus more transparent then than pot-metal, an advantage with dense colours like ruby and, later, blue and green. It was also possible to obtain rich patterns and subtle details by scratching away parts of the thin layer of coloured glass. This is known as *abrading*.

The second method of colouring was *staining*. In this process, discovered by the beginning of the fourteenth century, and known as *silver stain* or *yellow stain*, glass was painted with silver nitrate, then fired in an oven. According to the number of times the glass was stained then fired, a range of yellow tones varying from pale lemon to deep orange could be produced. This innovation simplified and revolutionised glass design, for it enabled different hues to be shown on the same piece of glass. Previously, when the artist wished to depict a golden crown, orange halo or fair hair on a white head, he had to cut out separate pieces of pot-metal in yellow and white and then lead them together. Now all he had to do was paint on the stain for the crown or hair, and draw the face, on one piece of white glass.

9. (Above) Ely Cathedral: Stained Glass Museum. Fourteenth-century silver-stain knight and peasant from the Lady Chapel in the cathedral, an example of the range of yellow tones obtained by the staining process

10. (Opposite page) St Mary, Stoke D'Abernon, Surrey. Sixteenth-century Flemish depiction of the angels appearing to the shepherds at the Nativity, showing painting with coloured enamels.

Details of faces, folds of clothes, background patterns, washes, shading and texturing were all painted on to the glass in medieval times with one dark pigment of copper or iron oxide mixed with soft powdered glass and wine or urine. This was then made permanent by firing in the kiln. But from the sixteenth century a whole range of coloured enamel pigments (made by finely grinding coloured glass) could be painted on to the same piece of glass and again made permanent by firing. Colour in glass was therefore achieved in three main ways: the molten process, by staining and by painting.

The only type of glass made in England until the sixteenth century was white glass and the chief centre was at Chiddingfold in Surrey. Glass was sold by the *wey* or *ponder*, a ponder weighing 5 pounds (2.268 kg). In the fourteenth century a ponder could cost from 6d to 9d. Coloured glass was imported from the continent. In the earlier Middle Ages there were two main places of manufacture, the Rhine valley and Normandy. Glass from the Rhine was shipped to such ports as Hull and glass from Normandy entered through one of the southern ports. The tendency was for glassmakers in the south to use the greenish Normandy glass and those in the north to use that from Germany. Normandy glass in the fourteenth century could cost from 6d a square foot and coloured 1s, while German coloured glass could cost from 2s 2d to 3s 7d a ponder, depending on the colour: at this stage blue glass seems to have been the most expensive.

How stained glass windows were made

The traditional way of lead-glazing is still followed by many studios. The first stage was for the preliminary design, known in medieval times as a *vidimus*, to be produced by the designer or workshop and approved by the patron. Then the window opening or *light* to be filled was measured precisely and a template or copy of the shape made. The design was then redrawn at the full size: this is still known as the *cartoon*. Medieval cartoons were originally made by drawing the design in charcoal on a trestle table which had been coated with whitewash; such a table has survived from Gerona Cathedral, Spain. Parchment and then paper were used later. Nowadays a strong cartridge paper is the most common material.

The cartoon included broad lines to indicate the lead strips which hold the pieces of glass and also indicated the colour of

11. Little Hampden, Buckinghamshire. Detail by M. C. Farrer Bell in the memorial window (1950) to his father (R. O. Bell), whom he designated as 'Bell, stained glass artist'. It represents a steel wheel cutter and pliers, for first cutting and then shaping a piece of glass.

each piece. Sheets of glass were then placed on top of the cartoon and cut to shape. (Today it is usual to make a tracing of the lead lines, called a cutline, to work from.) In medieval times the pieces of glass were given an approximate form by being scored with a hot iron and then plunged in water or by applying water or spit while the iron was on the glass. Then each piece was trimmed into shape with an iron tool like a pair of pliers called a *grozing-iron*. From the seventeenth century greater precision was achieved through the use of diamond cutters. Modern glaziers use a steel-wheeled cutter which makes a thin incision on the surface of the glass, which can then be gently divided manually.

The pieces of glass were then placed over the cartoon so that the details of the design could be painted in, copied from the drawing underneath. At first this was done purely in line but later on washes were used to show shadow and modify the light admitted. The brushes used were made from different animal hairs, mainly badger and hog. Paint was normally applied to the panel front (to be seen from inside the building). Silver staining was also done at this stage but it was applied to the back. The painted and stained pieces were then placed on a tray and fired in a kiln to fuse the paint permanently with the surface of the glass. Several stages of firing might be necessary. The correct temperatures and times for firing are crucial, otherwise textures will be uneven or the glass may crack. Even now, with sophisticated modern kilns run by gas or electricity, perfect results cannot be guaranteed, yet medieval craftsmen achieved their high standards in kilns made of clay, dung and hay plastered over a frame of wood or iron, heated to white heat by beech logs.

12. Leading a stained glass window at G. King & Son, Norwich. Below the glass is the *cutline*, or working drawing; completed sections are held in place temporarily by long nails; the small pliers near the craftsman's right hand are here used for stretching the lead cames.

13. Sealing the panel by working cement into the cracks with a stiff brush. The surplus is soaked up with sawdust and brushed off. Both sides are treated.

When the pieces of glass had cooled in the kiln they were laid out over the cartoon and fastened together with strips of lead, a relatively cheap, flexible yet durable metal. These strips are grooved with an H-shaped cross-section and are known as *calmes* or *cames* after the reeds (*calami* in Latin) which originally served as moulds for the molten lead. Leads were also made by scraping grooves in strips of lead. From the seventeenth century they were made in lead mills and are now mass-produced, although some studios still mill their own.

As each strip of lead was slotted over a piece of glass, it was held in place by *closing* or *clorying* nails until the next piece was inserted. When the whole panel was completed, the leads were soldered at each joint and on both sides with a wax flux; the medieval glazier used an iron heated in the furnace, but the modern soldering-iron is gas or electric. The whole panel was framed with wider strips of lead. A waterproof cement (powdered whitening, plaster of Paris, boiled linseed oil and lampblack) was worked with a stiff brush into all the gaps between lead and glass to make the window firm and weatherproof. The

14. Installing renovated window panels at St Mary, Bury St Edmunds, Suffolk.

15. Ely Cathedral: east window. Armature holding in place nineteenth-century glass by Wailes in the originally thirteenth-century setting.

glazier then soldered copper wires to the frame which would attach it to the bar which was to support it in the window frame.

Twentieth-century innovations include *copper-foiling*, in which very small pieces of glass are edged by copper tape and are then joined by soldering. The technique was invented by the American Louis C. Tiffany, in order to achieve the curved shapes of his distinctive lampshades. *Appliquéd glass* does not use lead either, but involves overlapping pieces of glass being held together by resins. The thick cast slabs of *dalle de verre* used to form walls of glass are normally set in concrete frames.

If the window opening, or lights is large, it will need several panels to fill it; these are supported by horizontal iron bars known as *saddle* bars, to which the panels are tied. In the twelfth and thirteenth centuries, glass was often held in place by external iron armatures bent to the shape of the panels which were to fill them: panels were fixed into them by eyelets and wedges. Surviving examples can be seen at Canterbury Cathedral.

These days the various stages of manufacture can be carried out by people specialising in the separate processes but working within a large studio; or a single craftsman may tackle most of the processes alone, or use an outside firm for leading or final installation. From the Middle Ages there is documentary evidence for the different roles and status of those involved in window production. The earliest window-makers were known by the Latin word for a glazier, *vitrarius*. By the twelfth century, this had changed to *verarius* or *verrarius*. Although glass was mainly commissioned by the monasteries, the craftsmen were not monks but laymen who had received a thorough training in the craft as apprentices in a workshop, their progress supervised by the master glazier. Because so many of the glaziers working here were French, thirteenth-century stained glass artists were often called *verrers* or *verrours* from *verre*, the French for glass. In the fourteenth century, when there were many more English craftsmen, these terms gave way to *glass wryghte* or *glasenwright*, from the Old English *wyrhta*, a worker. By the end of the century, this had been replaced by the titles *glasier* or *glasyer*. These names continued until the seventeenth century, when *glass painter* came into use. *Glass stainer* was also used from the eighteenth century, although the staining process had been in existence long before this. The modern term *lead glazier* refers specifically to the person who cuts, leads and instals the panels; designing and painting are not functions implied by this title. *Stained glass artist* is the term most commonly used now by those who design and paint panels.

Comparatively large numbers of people have been involved in making stained glass. About forty-five names are known from the period up to 1300, more than seventy-five in the fourteenth century, and over seventy in the fifteenth and sixteenth – and there must have been many more. Some of these people were no doubt jobbing craftsmen who supplied simple stained glass at a cheap rate, but the master glaziers of the larger firms were important men as well as being outstanding craftsmen. They were honoured by civic posts and the portrait of Thomas Glazier of Oxford was even included in a late fourteenth-century window at Winchester College (Hampshire) – a privilege usually reserved for the donor of the window.

Medieval glaziers formed themselves into guilds to regulate matters of work and to protect their interests – against foreign competition, for example. This proved a necessary precaution, because from about 1490 onwards both Henry VII and Henry VIII encouraged foreign craftsmen to live and work in England.

As early as the thirteenth century, there was an official known as King's Glazier, a post which, by the fifteenth century, carried with it an allowance of a shilling a day. The duties were to glaze and repair windows in any building belonging to the king or founded by him, though the holder could also take on other work if he wished.

The different hierarchies of work are shown by the rates paid for the different stages of production: for work at Westminster in 1351 the master glazier was paid 1s a day for drawing the design on the table (he might also be the designer). Those who cut the glass to shape received 6d a day, while those who painted the pieces before firing were of higher status and received 7d. Windows were costed at so much the square foot (30 by 30 cm), depending upon the quality of glass and other materials used: in the fourteenth century, 13d a square foot was paid for windows in Windsor Castle, while by the sixteenth century the price of good quality work had risen to 1s 4d and 1s 6d a square foot. But the price was variable and cheaper glass could be obtained. The highest recorded price was 2s a square foot paid to John Prudde, appointed King's Glazier in 1440, for the magnificent windows in the

16. New College, Oxford: chapel. Fourteenth-century figure of an angel by Thomas Glazier.

Beauchamp Chapel in St Mary's, Warwick, in 1447. As a contract could run into a thousand square feet or so of glass, furnishing a church with stained glass was an expensive business. Modern craftsmen still tend to charge by the square foot and it is still the quality of the glass employed, as well as the amount of painting, that determines the price.

In the Middle Ages there were great centres of manufacture at London, Oxford, Canterbury, Norwich, York and other cathedral cities. It was the strength of the medieval tradition, and the substantial amount of stained glass remaining, that helped the craft to survive the period of decline in the sixteenth and seventeenth centuries. York remained an important centre of glass painters, as did Norwich, and craftsmen drawing upon the skills of plumbing, china painting and decorating were on hand to produce the earliest Gothic Revival windows at the very beginning of the nineteenth century.

Such men worked individually, or with one or two assistants, but from the 1860s a large commercial studio would employ up to two hundred people, whose functions were as strictly demarcated as they had been in the Middle Ages. Some firms employed their own designers, who were often the partners; others employed freelance designers, who might therefore work for several different firms. Census returns reflect the increasing demand for windows in the nineteenth century: the figures are underestimated but, for 1831, only three people are recorded making stained glass, for 1841, 108, and for 1851, 531. The increase continued until 1870 and many large firms survived well into the twentieth century.

In England these days many stained glass artists work independently or in very small studios; by contrast, some of the larger cathedrals, such as York, Canterbury and Lincoln, have associated studios, whose main job is to look after the cathedral glass but which will also undertake outside commissions. Students can specialise in glass design, manufacture and conservation at some art colleges and then have to make the choice between setting up alone or becoming attached to an established studio. Stained glass is also widely taught at evening classes and summer schools.

There is just as much demand for the conservation and restoration of old windows as for the making of new ones. Although glass itself is extremely durable (apart from the deliberate vandalism that generates an increasing need for

17. St Mary, Warwick: Beauchamp Chapel, east window. Fifteenth-century windows made by John Prudde, the King's Glazier, 1447-50. The top row of figures represent St Thomas à Becket, St Alban, St Elizabeth, Isaiah, the Virgin Mary, St Winifred and St John of Bridlington. Glass 'jewels' to enhance the rich garments are set into drilled holes.

repairs), lead needs regular renewing and will not normally remain in sound condition for more than one hundred years. Therefore a programme of regular re-leading and cleaning to remove the general dirt and pollution is essential, although it can seldom be afforded by the smaller churches. The conservation and repair of medieval and later glass requires specialist skills; the establishment and maintenance of the necessary high standards is a crucial area in contemporary training. Modern conservators use complex scientific techniques and they must ensure that any treatment may be reversible in the future. They also have to decide whether missing portions should be replaced by modern replicas so convincing as to deceive the spectator or by more obviously recent panels.

3
The subject matter
of stained glass windows

Medieval windows

Stained glass artists of the Middle Ages drew upon a wide range of sources for their subjects. While only a small proportion of these would find their way into the windows of the ordinary parish church, the glass in the larger churches and in cathedrals was composed to portray an extensive selection of subjects. The building itself would suggest some of the themes, such as the saint or martyr with whom it was associated, or the donors who had commissioned the windows, who might appear as small figures at the foot of the window or in the tracery lights. Different locations within the church were traditionally filled by particular subjects: the east window by the Crucifixion, the west by the Last Judgement. There was no attempt at historical accuracy in the depiction of biblical scenes: medieval artists showed the things they knew, so that dress, armour, ships, buildings and interiors are all of their own time. It made the lessons of the windows more relevant to worshippers and ultimately has provided the modern spectator with a wealth of detail about daily life in the Middle Ages. Although a detailed knowledge of sources is not essential to enjoying stained glass, it helps to remove confusion if types of window can be identified.

Picture windows

Biblical history was interpreted in artistic terms as a series of links between the Old and the New Testament. Illustrated Bibles, such as *Speculum Humanae Salvationis* ('The Mirror of Man's Salvation') and *Biblia Pauperum* ('The Bible of the Poor') selected scenes from the Old Testament, called *type*, as events predicting and paralleling those from the New Testament, called *anti-type*. For example, Jonah emerging after three days in the belly of the whale was the type for the anti-type of the Resurrected Christ. These typological contrasts were followed in stained glass; the best-known examples are in the early thirteenth-century 'Theological' windows at Canterbury Cathedral, and in the sixteenth-century glass of King's College

18. St Mary, Westwood, Wiltshire: east window. Fifteenth-century 'Lily Crucifixion' – combining the Lily of the Annunciation with the Cross – flanked by eight angels carrying instruments of the Passion.

19. Dorchester Abbey, Oxfordshire. Unique fourteenth-century Tree of Jesse window in which the stone tracery forms the tree and its branches springing from the carved figure of Jesse at the base. Other figures are carved into the stonework. In the panels between are the remains of the stained glass figures.

chapel, Cambridge, where, in the two-tiered windows, the upper lights are Old Testament scenes and the lower New Testament.

The medieval bible which furnished these subjects was the Vulgate edition, so called from the Latin word *vulgata*, meaning 'popular'. This was a fourth-century translation into Latin of the Hebrew Old Testament and the Greek New Testament. It is still the authorised version of the Roman Catholic Church.

The Old Testament provided many stories suitable for picture windows. In the fourteenth and fifteenth centuries especially, the stories of the Creation, of Adam and Eve, the Flood, and histories of Abraham, Jacob, Joseph, Moses and Aaron were common. These stories were often made into a series; there is an outstanding example at Great Malvern Priory (Worcestershire), where in the south chancel thirty-three panels still survive from the original seventy-two. Other series or part-series remain at Barkway (Hertfordshire), Thaxted (Essex), St Neot (Cornwall), Hereford Cathedral and Lincoln Cathedral.

New Testament windows were usually based on the **Life of Christ**, which could be prefaced by the birth and upbringing of Mary, starting with the story of Christ's grandparents, Joachim and Anna. These stories would be taken from the Apocryphal gospels of the second century, which, after centuries of rejection, had now come to be part of the Catholic tradition. Phases of Christ's life were depicted, including the Annunciation and Nativity, the Miracles, scenes of the Passion, Crucifixion, Resurrection and the Acts of the Apostles. Cycles of the Life of the Virgin were also extremely popular.

The type of window known as the **Tree of Jesse** was very prominent. This illustrated the antecedents of Christ, tracing his descent from Jesse, the father of David. The window was literally a picture of a family tree. Jesse was positioned at the bottom of the window, and from him rose a vine which could spread right across the window, ignoring the stone frames. The decorated stem was twisted into ovals, each one containing the splendid figure of one of Jesse's descendants. Kings were arranged up the trunk, sometimes with the addition of the prophets, who told of Christ's coming, on the outside. At the top of the tree were Mary and the infant Christ or Christ on His throne. There are twelfth-century fragments of the subject at York Minster and Canterbury Cathedral, good fourteenth-century examples at St Mary's, Shrewsbury, and Wells Cathedral, and fifteenth-century ones at Margaretting (Essex) and Leverington (Cambridgeshire).

20. Selby Abbey, North Yorkshire. Much restored Tree of Jesse window, *c.*1330, in the style of Master Robert of York. The family tree of Christ grows out of the sleeping Jesse, His ancestor.

The **Last Judgement** or **Doom** was another major subject; it was usually given an important position either in the large east window or, more commonly, the west window. Sometimes it is found in the tracery lights of Jesse windows, as in Wells Cathedral and Winchester College chapel.

This subject matter gave great scope for the artist's invention, but always followed the same general layout. The lower part of the window is given over to the souls who, having risen from their graves, are being weighed in the balance by St Michael. Some pass St Peter and enter heaven; most are dragged off to the torments of hell, which are shown vividly. Kings, popes and bishops are often among the damned, being burnt by lurid flames or tortured by grotesque demons – no soul was saved by virtue of his office, but only by being good. Above all this rises Christ in Majesty, flanked by the Virgin Mary and St John. The Apostles may also be included, and the traceries are often filled by angels summoning the dead. There are good examples at Fairford (Gloucestershire), Tewkesbury Abbey (Gloucestershire) and Ticehurst (East Sussex).

21. St Mary, Fairford, Gloucestershire: west window. Christ presides over the Last Judgement; below Him St Michael weighs the souls of the dead. Late fifteenth century.

Another narrative subject is the series of panels depicting the **Seven Sacraments**. These were: Baptism, Confirmation, Marriage, Penance, Holy Orders, Holy Communion, and Last Rites. They could be arranged around the figure of Christ crucified or risen, each sacrament receiving a stream of blood from his wounds. There are imperfect fifteenth-century examples at Crudwell (Wiltshire), Doddiscombsleigh (Devon) and Tattershall (Lincolnshire).

There were also the **Seven Works of Mercy**: Feeding the Hungry, Giving Drink to the Thirsty, Clothing the Naked, Housing the Stranger, Visiting the Sick, Visiting Prisoners and Burying the Dead. These can be seen at Chinnor (Oxfordshire), Combs (Suffolk) and Tattershall (Lincolnshire), and a seventeenth-century enamel painted series can be seen at Messing (Essex).

A striking fifteenth-century window at St Andrew's church, Norwich, shows the **Dance of Death**, a common scene in medieval art and a subject perhaps made relevant by the Black Death of 1348-50. Death leads all kinds of men off to his kingdom in a macabre dance.

Figure windows

These showed single standing figures, or groups of such figures, placed in separate lights. Pictures of saints were very popular. There were around four thousand saints to choose from, including many hardly known now. They are usually shown holding an emblem and, particularly from the fourteenth century onwards, their names are often written in Latin, such as *Egidius* for Giles, *Jacobus* for James, *Hieronymus* for Jerome, and so on. They could also be recognised by particular attributes associated with their life or death: St Catherine carries the wheel that she was tortured on and the sword which beheaded her; St Lawrence holds the gridiron on which he was burned to death.

Many of them were patron saints and protectors and were shown several times in the same church. St Christopher was particularly popular because anyone who looked at his image was supposed to be safe from sudden death on that day. Various saints were believed to be able to protect suppliants against disease or misfortune: St Lucy (with a sword through her neck) against eye diseases, St Roch (with a plague spot on his leg) against the plague and St Apollonia (with pincers and a tooth) against toothache. It was this kind of belief that was later

22. St Andrew, Norwich. Fifteenth-century Dance of Death; Death takes away a bishop.

23. All Saints, Hillesden, Buckinghamshire: south transept, east window. The story of St Nicholas in an early sixteenth-century foreign portrayal of the *Golden Legend*.

denounced as superstitious and used as a reason for the destruction of windows. Others were patron saints: St Nicholas (three children in a tub) of children, sailors, thieves and pawnbrokers, St Catherine of schools and learning. To stress their importance, saints were dressed in rich, formal vestments, and not the everyday wear of many other figures.

The **Lives of the Saints**, with their miracles and martyrdoms, were also depicted as picture windows in some of the larger churches. The windows were generally based on the account of the lives of the saints in the *Golden Legend*, a popular book

24. (Opposite) Lincoln Cathedral: north transept. The tracery of the Bishop's Eye rose window contains many fragments of fourteenth-century glass; the lancets below, portraying many stories, are of the thirteenth century.

25. Victoria and Albert Museum, London. Angel playing a rebeck, fifteenth century.

originally compiled in Latin by a friar in the thirteenth century, then published in English by Caxton in 1483. Its author had called it *Legends of the Saints* but it came to be called the *Golden Legend* because of people's respect for it.

The **Nine Orders of Angels** were often shown, especially in traceries. They were categorised into three groups, which could be depicted in a great variety of ways. The first group consisted of Seraphim, Cherubim and Thrones, all supporting and worshipping God's Throne. The second were the Governors of the Universe – Dominations, Virtues and Powers. The third group were Principalities, Archangels and Angels – the Messengers of God's Will. They were frequently shown with musical instruments and feathered garments.

The **Twelve Apostles** and **Twelve Prophets** were also used to make series of figure windows. By tradition, the Apostles were supposed to have contributed one clause each to the Creed, which became the canon of the Catholic religion. So each figure is shown holding an emblem, and also a scroll on which is written his article of the Creed. Thus St Peter stands with his keys of gold and silver and the text: *Credo in Deum Patrem Omnipotentem creatorem coeli et terrae* – 'I believe in God the Father Almighty, maker of heaven and earth'. There is an intact medieval series at Fairford (Gloucestershire) and complete seventeenth-century series at Wadham College and Lincoln College, Oxford. Many churches have incomplete series.

The Twelve Prophets were designed as a parallel to the series of Apostles. They were never named or given emblems, but they, too, carry scrolls, this time with a quotation from the Old Testament. Obadiah, for example, carries the inscription: *Et erit regnum Domini, Amen* – 'And the Kingdom shall be the Lord's, Amen'. Once again, there is a perfect series at Fairford.

26. Selsley, Gloucestershire. A medallion of the lion of St Mark designed by Philip Webb, 1861.

The **Four Evangelists** may surround Christ and may be accompanied or represented by their symbols, an angel for St Matthew, a lion for St Mark, a calf for St Luke and an eagle for St John.

Rose windows

The symbolic significance of numbers in medieval art is examplified in the great round, or rose, windows in cathedrals. These combined the geometric perfection of the circle, symbolising the universe, or eternity, with mathematically complex internal divisions created by stone mullions in the form of wheel spokes, petals or flames. The numbers seven, nine and twelve were especially significant to theologians, and appropriate figures were arranged in series to reach these totals. The subject portrayed in the glass filling the apertures is dominated by the design; it can combine a central figure, such as Christ or the Virgin and Child, with outer tiers of angels or apostles interspersed with purely decorative panels. The thirteenth-century rose window known as the 'Dean's Eye' at Lincoln Cathedral has the Last Judgement as its main theme.

Post-medieval windows

The change in religious attitudes in the sixteenth century brought to an end the formerly consistent schemes of medieval windows. New subjects less associated with Roman Catholicism were necessary: these included secular scenes, taken from literary, particularly classical, sources, a greater emphasis on

27. Victoria and Albert Museum, London. The wedding of St George and the Princess (after the saint had killed the dragon), designed by D. G. Rossetti for Morris & Co in 1862.

28. Bisham, Berkshire. Heraldic glass of 1609.

donor portraits, and an expansion of heraldry. Stained glass was an ideal medium for heraldic images, as the bright colours and bold delineation were ideal for illustrating coats of arms. Heraldic windows were appropriate not only for churches but also for civic and domestic buildings and as glass began to be increasingly used in such settings, rather than in purely religious ones, biblical subjects became less relevant.

Small portable panels made of a single piece of glass painted with detailed scenes of daily life, often copied from book engravings, were produced on a large scale in the Netherlands and Germany. Many such roundels were imported to England and installed in churches and other buildings, as at Stoke D'Abernon (Surrey) and Erpingham (Norfolk).

During the seventeenth and eighteenth centuries heraldic subjects remained popular and there were also secular scenes, including portraits of royalty.

During the Gothic Revival, when Victorian craftsmen copied directly many of the religious subjects of medieval glass, there were new themes as well. Illustrations of medieval literature and history were popular with the Pre-Raphaelite designers, such as the depiction of Chaucer's women characters in the Combination Room at Peterhouse, Cambridge, and in the later nineteenth century panels of flowers and plants were installed in many private houses. By the end of the century the Art Nouveau movement was for the first time using abstract de-

29. Daresbury, Cheshire. Memorial windows (1932) to Lewis Carroll (Charles Lutwidge Dodgson), born in the vicarage there in 1832, designed by Geoffrey Webb in the style of Carroll's illustrator, Tenniel.

30. Helpringham, Lincolnshire. Detail of a window of 1940 which shows how modern designers supply contemporary details just as medieval designers did.

signs, for example in the Willow Tea Rooms in Glasgow, designed by C. R. Mackintosh, as well as non-figural land-scapes and foliage designs. However, there was also a greater realism in figure painting on glass, reflecting the influence of photography. The expanding secular demand is shown in the sequence of sportsmen in the windows of the Café Royal in Edinburgh designed by Tom Wilson.

In the twentieth century, both abstract and realistic windows have been required. Non-figural windows are increasingly com-missioned for churches because of the belief that spirituality can be inspired by the symbolism of pure pattern and colour as well as by the biblical narratives of the past. Examples can be seen in the glass at Liverpool Roman Catholic, Coventry and Manchester cathedrals. However, the more familiar Bible sub-jects survive, showing the great strength of the medieval tradi-tion. Literary subjects include the Tenniel illustrations of *Alice in Wonderland* in Daresbury (Cheshire) and Christ Church Hall, Oxford. There are realistic portrait windows of George VI and his family in Canterbury Cathedral. First and Second World War memorial windows include details of individuals, their uniforms and weapons, and battle grounds.

4
The historical development of stained glass

The twelfth century

Only a very small proportion of the glass installed in Britain in the twelfth century survives because most was replaced as a result of subsequent changes in taste and alterations to buildings. However, what may be a late eleventh-century window is still in position at Dalbury (Derbyshire).

Romanesque window openings were generally single, with rounded arches. Much of the glass which survives of the period is in Canterbury Cathedral, where it was installed after 1184 when the cathedral was rebuilt in the new French Gothic style; most of it is no longer in its original position. There are smaller amounts of English glass at Dorchester Abbey (Oxfordshire), Brabourne (Kent) and York Minster. There are also panels of imported French glass at Rivenhall (Essex), Wilton (Wiltshire) and Twycross (Leicestershire).

There is a superb series of **figure** windows at Canterbury, showing the ancestry of Christ. Thirty-eight remain from the original eighty-four; they are now in the south transept and nave, having first been installed in the clerestory (the upper level of the nave). Each light contains two figures with names inscribed, set one above the other. They are seated on thrones surmounted by simple arches or canopies. The figures have an alertness, dignity and simplicity of drawing that places them among the greatest achievements of stained glass, in spite of the fact that hands and feet have often been badly restored and many borders have been removed. These borders ran right around the window frame and were 7 or 8 inches (18 or 20 cm) wide. They were finely drawn and of unparalleled richness of colour and design.

Also at Canterbury are fine examples of **medallion** windows. These originate in the very late twelfth or early thirteenth century and show incidents and groups of figures set in circular- or square-framed medallions. A number of such medallions

31. (Opposite page) Canterbury Cathedral: south-west transept. Ancestors of Christ, late twelfth century.

32.
Canterbury
Cathedral:
south
transept.
Methu-
selah,
one of
the
ancestors
of Christ,
twelfth
century.
These
massive
figures
were
designed
to be
seen at a
great
height.

go to make up a window, each surrounded by thin borders of glass decorated with formalised leaf patterns in contrasting colours to those of the medallions. The whole arrangement is surrounded by a wider border. The designs were created like a mosaic, in strong, intense colours, with much ruby and blue. Often as many as a hundred different pieces of glass could be used in a medallion only one foot (30 cm) across, giving an ornate and jewel-like effect.

The setting of an incident is shown in a symbolic, stylised way: there is no attempt at realism. Outdoor scenes are suggested by a tree or building, indoor ones by arches. Artists at this time were not concerned with creating the illusions of scale or perspective. The painting was in line only and the brushwork was sensitive yet vigorous. Figures show exaggerated gestures and their faces are given the compelling quality of an icon – an effect achieved at Canterbury by wide open eyes with the pupils shown as large black dots. Haloes are always formed from a separate piece of glass.

What was happening in the medallion was often explained by a Latin inscription. An area of the glass was covered with the dark paint used for drawing and the letters were scratched out of this with a sharp stick. The chunky majuscule lettering used at this time is called *Lombardic*, which is far easier to read than

33. (Below) Church of the Nativity of the Virgin, Madley, Herefordshire: thirteenth-century east window. Medallions depicting John in the bosom of Christ at the Last Supper and the Adoration of the Magi.

the tall, narrow black-letter *Gothic* script which took its place later. The medallion windows at Canterbury are in the north choir aisle and show Old and New Testament subjects from the *Biblia Pauperum*. There is also an example at Dorchester Abbey (Oxfordshire), based on the life of St Birinus.

Simple versions of the family tree of Christ, or **Jesse** windows, survive from this time. The panels at York Minster (*c*.1150) and at Canterbury (thirteenth-century) both show the strong influence of French glass, for the theme had been invented at St Denis, near Paris, the first fully Gothic building. (In Wilton parish church, Wiltshire, there are some reset twelfth-century panels from St Denis.)

The only surviving example of an early **rose** window is in the north-east transept at Canterbury (although it is incomplete). The subject is the Old Law, and the window originally showed Moses, the Cardinal Virtues and the Great and Minor Prophets – an ambitious scheme.

Grisaille was a cheaper and simpler form of glass painting, in which clear or white glass was painted (in black paint) with foliage or geometric designs. The name comes from the French *grisailler*, meaning to paint grey. It was first developed in the twelfth century as a result of the more austere approach to church decoration of the Cistercian order, which had forbidden the use of coloured or figured glass. But as it was also much cheaper to produce it was popular in the smaller parish churches. The earliest known panel in England is in Brabourne (Kent).

The thirteenth century

Rounded Romanesque windows were gradually replaced by the pointed forms of the Early English phase of the English Gothic architectural sequence. These single narrow windows are called *lancets*, and the new shape affected the design of the stained glass filling it. Later in the century two or more lancets might be placed side by side.

In **medallion** windows there was now rather more emphasis on detailed drawing. The beautiful all-over designs in geometric or foliage shapes used in backgrounds were known as *diaper* patterns; these were obtained by scratching through a matt wash of the dark oxide paint. The borders all round the windows became thinner and were, perhaps, less inventive in design. New subjects were added, in particular the lives of the saints. There is a fine series *c*.1220 showing the life of St

34. York Minster: north transept. *Grisaille* glass of *c*.1260, the pieces painted with foliage patterns, fills the tall lancets of the 'Five Sisters'.

Thomas à Becket and miracles associated with him in the Trinity Chapel at Canterbury (see page 9).

Fragments only of **figure** windows survive from the thirteenth century; there are examples in the north, south and east choir aisles of Lincoln Cathedral.

Grisaille windows became increasingly popular after the middle of the century, when lighter interiors began to be preferred to the glowing but dim atmosphere created by ruby and blue pot-metal glass. The leaves drawn with black oxide became more realistic, although still stylised. The background was often cross-hatched. Another type of grisaille window consisted of complicated geometrical patterns of interlaced strapwork heightened by colour. When used for borders, foliage often alternated with pieces of plain coloured glass. At this time the leaf patterns were confined to each separate pane of glass, but later they were so arranged as to suggest that they were straying from panel to panel, as tendrils wind around a trellis. A fine example is the glass in the five huge lancets at York Minster c.1260, known as the 'Five Sisters'.

In order to adapt to the long thin shape of a lancet, towards the end of the thirteenth century artists started placing in the window a single row of vertical medallions filled with grisaille glass. The shape of the medallions varied: they could be circles, oblongs with trefoil heads, quatrefoils or pointed ovals. These were both cheaper and more luminous than entire medallion windows and more interesting than plain grisaille ones.

Foliage grisaille was more popular than the strapwork kind for these windows. The medallions often contained single figures – saints or apostles, for example – with the first hints of the graceful, draped S-shaped posture which was to become characteristic of fourteenth-century work. The medallions are simpler than the earlier ones and made of larger pieces of glass, which can be seen especially in the drapery, which has fewer folds. The flesh colour was much lighter and hair was drawn on the same piece of glass as the face rather than on a separate, differently coloured piece. Haloes were still separate.

Another variation, which started around 1270, was the **heraldic** window. The brightly coloured shields were pointed and curved and contained only one coat of arms, placed against

35. (Opposite page) Wells Cathedral, Somerset: Lady Chapel. An angel from a fourteenth-century Doom reset here.

grisaille at the bottom of a window. The earliest surviving shields are now in the west window of Salisbury Cathedral, although they were made for the chapter-house.

Parts of **Tree of Jesse** windows survive at Salisbury Cathedral, Lincoln Minster and Westwell (Kent). From these it can be seen that the delineation of drapery, figures and vines had become more flowing. The tree generally filled only one lancet. The colour of the ovals containing the figures was often counterchanged with that of the background panels, the usual contrast being blue and ruby.

The main **rose** window remaining from this period is the 'Dean's Eye' at Lincoln, although it is patched in places with other thirteenth-century glass. It is 24 feet (7.3 metres) across.

The fourteenth century

From about 1250 architectural style had been developing into the Decorated period of English Gothic architecture marked by much larger windows, divided by stone mullions into two or more tall, narrow lights. These had *trefoil* or *cinquefoil* heads surmounted by increasingly elaborate tracery lights. The geometrical iron armatures which had supported the medallions of the twelfth and thirteenth centuries gave way to vertical iron supports, or *saddle bars*.

Designs for windows had to be adapted to suit the expanding areas to be filled. **Figure-and-canopy** windows became the most typical windows of the period, in which a standing figure was placed under a complicated architectural canopy resembling those in stone sculpture, tombs and brasses. These forms became more and more elaborate and could occupy much of the upper part of the window. The graceful S-pose for such figures (see opposite) became increasingly characteristic and they were often unnaturally elongated in order to fill the long spaces available. The great east window at Gloucester, *c.*1357, has rows of such figures under canopies, representing the Coronation of the Virgin, while the west window of York Minster shows bishops and apostles. At first, architectural details in the canopies were scraped out of the background of black paint, but later silver-stained white glass became popular. By the end of the century figures stood on bases such as tiled pavements.

Coloured figure-and-canopy panels were generally placed halfway up the lights, the rest of the windows being filled with grisaille set off by a shield or roundel. The panels thus made a

36. Ely Cathedral: Stained Glass Museum. Annunciation, *c.*1340, from Hadzor, Worcestershire.

band of colour separating two white zones. Sometimes, instead of a single figure a simple group of figures based on biblical subjects was shown under a canopy. Backgrounds were often coloured and richly diapered. Borders became narrow and made up of motifs such as fleurs-de-lis or oak sprigs, alternating with blocks of red or blue glass. This kind of border was comparatively mechanical but still attractive.

Saints are often shown with their emblems, such as St Catherine with her wheel at Deerhurst (Gloucestershire). In many cases hair and folds of a garment are drawn with a beautiful rhythmic flow. Smeared paint shading is occasionally used for faces, but as yet the modelling is tentative. The general use of pattern in the best decorative work is extraordinarily assured and satisfying. From this time onwards, the figure of the donor is often shown kneeling in prayer at the foot of the window.

The technique was discovered of silver-staining glass to produce tones of yellow in selected areas (see page 19). This meant, for example, that it was no longer necessary to cut a separate piece of glass for a halo. As the century progressed, the colour and texture of glass lost some of its richness, which was more appropriate for the larger, lighter buildings. Yellow and green grew in popularity at the expense of blue and ruby. White glass became clearer and tended to replace the pink-brown glass previously used for flesh. Coloured glass was often decorated with scratched diaper patterns, which were based on foliage and show great imagination: one pattern based on seaweed was particularly popular. Leaves and plants were more realistically drawn. The amount of heraldry in windows also greatly increased during this century. After 1375 came the change to Gothic black-letter script and the letters were now painted in black pigment; Latin is often used for dedications. *Scs* (Sanctus) denotes a male saint, *Sca* (Sancta) a female one. *Pph* shows a prophet.

In **grisaille** windows cross-hatched backgrounds disappeared and the leaf shapes became recognisable as vine, ivy, hawthorn, oak and other plants. They were no longer restricted to individual panels of glass but were allowed to grow in sprays over the whole window. Silver stain was used to enrich these leaf designs and further interest was added by small shields or roundels, or with emblems such as the keys of St Peter, or the popular medieval legend and symbol of Christ's sacrifice, the pelican wounding herself so that her young could drink her blood. There are some attractive shields at Tewkesbury Abbey and Gloucester Cathedral. Involved strapwork designs were succeeded by simpler arrangements of *quarries* (French *carreau*), lozenge- or diamond-shaped pieces of glass, as in Merton College chapel, Oxford.

A direct development from the medallion and grisaille window of the thirteenth century was the type of window showing **panels and single figures** on grisaille. Treatment of the medallions was the same as for figure and canopy panels. The Virgin and Child was an especially popular subject, such as that at Fladbury (Worcestershire), as also were scriptural ones, like scenes of the Nativity or Passion of Christ. Single figures could also be put straight on to a decorated quarry background (as became frequent in the fifteenth and sixteenth centuries) and this was a useful background for the figures of donors.

There are some fine examples of **Jesse** windows from this period. The vine could now cover up to seven lights, as the design ignored the mullions, and was now more naturalistic. The oval backgrounds to the figures were filled up with diaper patterns, different in colour to the background of the scroll. There are examples at Madley (Herefordshire), Wells Cathedral (Somerset) and Selby Abbey (North Yorkshire).

Tracery lights were filled with foliage patterns, grotesque beasts, angels, human heads with their names, saints, or even picture subjects, such as the Death of Becket window in Christ Church Cathedral, Oxford (figure 37). The symbols of the Four Evangelists and shields were also used. Towards the end of the century more diaper patterns and silver stain appear as backgrounds in traceries. In both the fourteenth and the fifteenth centuries angels are shown in two ways: in one they wear white robes, and in the other their bodies are covered with gold feathers such as were seen on angels in performances of miracle plays; the players' use of gesture and costumes were also reflected in stained glass, since poses and facial expressions were becoming generally more realistic. It was at this time that the process of *abrading* was first used on flash glass to reveal a second layer of colour on the same piece.

The **rose** window known as the Bishop's Eye, in Lincoln Cathedral, is no longer in its original condition but contains many fragments of fourteenth-century glass.

37. Christ Church Cathedral, Oxford: Lucy Chapel, east window. St Thomas à Becket is portrayed in the tracery; below are Saints Martin, Augustine, Blaise and Cuthbert (1320).

38. Victoria and Albert Museum, London. Head of a monk, fifteenth century. The face has been repaired subsequently.

The fifteenth century

Large, squarish Perpendicular windows, divided by horizontal and vertical elements, offered further scope for the designers. By this time, too, the wealthy and expanding middle classes could afford to install in their churches vast amounts of stained glass and much more has survived than from previous centuries. The main change in style is an increasing emphasis on drawing skills, which were starting to take precedence over those of glazing, except when small pieces of pot-metal were laboriously set into shields or the hems of clothes to represent jewels; John Prudde made outstanding examples in the Beauchamp Chapel in Warwick church. More white glass was used, which towards the end of the century acquired a delicate, silvery quality. The leads stopped playing such an important part in the design and began to be regarded as an irrelevance rather than the linear feature that they should properly be. The drawing, however, was detailed, subtle and crisp.

Quarry windows, which were an extension of grisaille windows, were great favourites at this time. The small diamond-shaped panels were individually decorated with stained motifs which included flowers, insects, leaves, birds and heraldic devices. They were varied and beautifully drawn: the Zouche Chapel at York Minster has some delightful birds. All-over leaf patterns were abandoned. Quarries still provided a background for figures, shields, roundels and strap borders as before.

Tiers of **figures-and-canopies** are the windows most frequently found in the fifteenth century. The figures began to be drawn more realistically, losing the S-pose. The faces are finely drawn, with stipple, smear and line used to suggest shadow and form and hence greater realism. Highlights are obtained by scratching through the smear. Hair was usually stained yellow, but haloes were still sometimes leaded separately. The canopies become increasingly fantastic, with pinnacles which make the windows look like grottoes festooned with icicles. There are good examples of figure-and-canopy windows at New College chapel, Oxford, and in various churches in York and Norwich, both of which were important centres of glazing, and the names of master glaziers, such as Thomas of Oxford and John Thornton of York, are increasingly recorded

Subject windows were also extremely popular, drawing upon many of the familiar biblical themes and lives of the saints. The scenes were arranged in rows across the lights, each one having its own canopy, until a change in taste later in the century when the canopy was left out. The east window at East Harling (Norfolk) has scenes from the Life of the Virgin, and that at St Peter Mancroft, Norwich, of the Life of Christ. Sometimes descriptions or articles from the Creed were written in black-letter script between the rows. Another new development was that subject windows started to spread over two or three lights, ignoring the mullions – as in the subject of the Crucifixion.

The demand for **Jesse** windows declined and few fifteenth-century examples remain; there is good one at Margaretting (Essex), where the figures in the ovals are in pairs.

Tracery lights remained very important, with more angels, sometimes holding shields. Heraldry was a flourishing subject, and this is the century of the donor in stained glass. Whole families are shown, kneeling in prayer and arranged in rows behind each other. They are shown on an increasingly large scale and can sometimes form the main subject of the windows, as at Long Melford (Suffolk).

There was also an increasing demand for secular stained glass; glaziers were employed to install heraldic windows or small roundels in manor houses and civic buildings.

39. (Opposite page) St Peter Mancroft, Norwich: east window. A wall of glass showing the Life of Christ and the saints.

40. (Left) Haddon Hall, Derbyshire: chapel. Fifteenth-century St Michael trampling on the Devil against a background of quarries.

42. (Opposite page) St Peter and St Paul, East Harling, Norfolk. Deposition c.1480.

41. (Below) Holy Trinity, Goodramgate, York: east window. Saints George, John the Baptist and the Virgin and the Corpus Christi, c.1470.

43. Canterbury Cathedral: north-west transept. Edward IV, a detail from the Royal window, 1476, by the King's Glazier, showing the royal family with saints and apostles.

The sixteenth century

By the end of the fifteenth century simplicity, strength and brilliance were gradually being lost from stained glass; during the sixteenth century they disappeared. This was largely due to the influence of the art of the Renaissance, which was man-orientated, not god-orientated, and it therefore clashed with the awe-inspiring art of stained glass in a very fundamental way. Renaissance artists were interested in the material world: anatomy was studied and perspective mastered. These preoccupations affected stained glass design: the types of window stayed the same but the treatment was very different.

Figures were more realistic and were set in solid-looking landscapes, complete with buildings, skies and trees; or else they were surrounded by interiors filled with their belongings and furniture. A clutter of objects seems to press in on the figures: there is pride in their possessions and virtuosity in their presentation. The result is a materialistic quality that is quite in contrast to that of medieval stained glass. Shading is produced by heavy stippling – a cruder and more mechanical effect than that produced by line drawing. Stained glass began to imitate contemporary painting: mullions were now consistently ignored and the window was treated as a whole. Some of the finest examples are at Fairford in Gloucestershire in the Crucifixion (east window) and the Last Judgement (west window).

Canopies are heavier and clumsier. Architecture is a mixture of Gothic and classical, including features such as fluted columns, architraves, scrollwork, cupids and garlands. Many of these features can be seen in King's College chapel, Cambridge, where all the sixteenth-century windows have survived.

Much work was commissioned from glaziers from Germany or the Netherlands, who settled in England in order to supply the more sophisticated demands of the court. Their designs were often based on drawings, woodcuts and engravings by leading continental artists.

These tendencies for stained glass to imitate paintings and drawings were further stimulated about the middle of the century when it was discovered that coloured glass paints, or enamels, could be made from powdered coloured glass mixed with borax, and that when it was fired it fused with the surface of the glass. There was no longer any need to cut separate shapes in glass and leadwork thus lost most of its importance as an element of design.

45. (Above) Peterhouse, Cambridge: chapel, east window. Crucifixion by Bernard van Linge *c*.1632.

44. (Opposite page) Stradsett, Norfolk. Sixteenth-century Adoration of the Magi made in Augsburg, Germany.

It was in **heraldic** work that the essential qualities of the craft were maintained. Shields were often complicated and contained a large number of quarterings of family arms. Since religious glass was virtually banned after the Reformation (although some was still made for private chapels), heraldic glass was in great demand.

The seventeenth century

At first, painting with the new enamel paints was used to supplement the more traditional techniques. This is the case with the heraldic panels made by Dininckhoff of York (c.1585), some of which can be seen at Gilling Castle (North Yorkshire). There was an increasing tendency towards great elaboration and realistic detail, as in the work late in the century of another York glazier, Henry Gyles (1645-1709), who was famous both for heraldic panels and for sundials.

Because of the destruction in the 1630s by Louis XIII of the glassworks in Lorraine, pot-metal became unobtainable and enamel paints came into their own. White glass was simply cut into rectangles and the leads which held them together became a grid which was ignored in the pictorial design. Oxford is the best place to study the glass of this period. Wadham, Lincoln, Balliol, Christchurch and University colleges all have examples of the work of Bernard and Abraham van Linge, German brothers who introduced continental styles to England in a phase of religious revival under Charles I. Their detailed painting and bright colours can also be seen at Peterhouse, Cambridge, and Lydiard Tregoze (Wiltshire). There is also a massive window of Old Testament scenes painted by French, Dutch and English artists at Hatfield House (Hertfordshire).

There are attractive portraits on glass by Richard Greenbury in several Oxford colleges, including Charles I and Henrietta Maria at Magdalene College. Another famous glass painter was Baptista Sutton, whose work can be seen in the Chapel of the Holy Trinity, Guildford.

There are remains of biblical scenes at Abbey Dore and Sellack (Herefordshire) but much glass of the period belongs to the category of painted domestic glass. Quarries and roundels were painted with a great variety of charming pictures and stained glass sundials were common. A fly was painted on many of them – a pictorial pun on the motto *Dum spectas fugio* ('Even as you watch, I fly'). Henry Gyles charged £1 for a sundial!

The eighteenth century

While stained glass in the seventeenth century had been mostly heraldic in character, in the eighteenth century there was a renewed demand for pictorial windows. Stained glass was now thought of in terms of a translucent oil painting and only very rarely was lead used to follow the outlines of the drawing. The white glass made at this time was exceptionally thin.

The influence of York continued through the work of the Price family: William Price the Elder, who had been trained by Henry Gyles, painted several windows in Oxford colleges, including the great east window of Merton College, now removed to the Stained Glass Museum at Ely. His son, Joshua,

46. Ely Cathedral: Stained Glass Museum. Detail of the Last Supper by William Price the Elder (1702), formerly in the east window of Merton College chapel, Oxford.

47. St Anne, Manchester: north aisle. The apostles Peter, James and John by William Peckitt, late eighteenth century.

incorporated some of the seventeenth-century panels by Abraham van Linge in his glazing scheme for Queen's College chapel, and also carried out Francisco Slater's designs for a fine series of windows now in Great Witley church (Worcestershire). William Price the Younger tried to work in a more medieval style and even attempted to manufacture coloured glass in order to achieve a more authentic effect. His windows of the 1730s and 1740s survive at New, Wadham and Magdalene Colleges, Oxford.

From the middle of the century William Peckitt of York (1731-95) was the leading figure in stained glass. Profoundly interested in the lost techniques of making medieval glass, he was successful in producing a type of 'flashed' ruby glass in the 1780s, but most Georgian glass painters preferred to achieve coloured effects by using enamel paints. In 1771 Peckitt painted a fine Last Supper window at Audley End (Essex) from designs by Biagio Rebecca, and his work can also be seen at St Martin-cum-Gregory, York, and in the famous Alma Mater window in the library of Trinity College, Cambridge, after an oil painting by Giovanni Cipriani.

In the later part of the century the most accomplished glass painters were Francis Eginton of Birmingham and James Pearson, who came to London from Dublin. Eginton's masterpiece is the Conversion of St Paul east window of St Paul's, Birmingham (1789), designed by the American painter Benjamin West: dark and dramatic, it demonstrates Eginton striving for a deliberately theatrical effect. Equally theatrical, but this time light and delicate in tone, is his east window of St Alkmund's, Shrewsbury (1782), the design of which was taken from Guido Reni's 'Assumption of the Virgin' (see figure 15). The largest and boldest surviving window by Pearson is his 'Moses and the Brazen Serpent', adapted from a painting by J. H. Mortimer, in the upper east window at Salisbury Cathedral. Pearson was also famous for his heraldic work. It is clear how dependent these glass painters were on the designs of established oil painters. The most renowned example of this sort of collaboration was the ante-chapel windows of New College, Oxford, showing the Nativity and the Virtues, made by Thomas Jervais in 1777-83 from the designs of Sir Joshua Reynolds, the leading academician of the day. The resulting panels were criticised because they represented a style which was becoming old-fashioned and which was seen as the antithesis of medieval glass. Yet the window, viewed on its own terms, is dramatic and intriguing, and a fine product of its time.

48. Crowland Abbey, Lincolnshire: east window. A nineteenth-century
copy of thirteenth-century glass in the choir of Canterbury Cathedral.

The nineteenth century

The rapid growth of population in the nineteenth century, the construction of many hundreds of new churches as a result of the 1818 Church Building Act, the effects of the Anglo-Catholic revival of worship, and the Gothic Revival of architecture were all factors which inspired a vast increase in the demand for new stained glass. An unprecedented volume of windows was made for buildings both in Britain and in other countries. It has been calculated that over eighty thousand windows were installed in England in the period, so the production of stained glass became a flourishing industry. Considering the quantity of work for which the larger studios were responsible, it is remarkable that standards remained as high as they did, although later in the century there was a tendency for their approach to become stereotyped and mechanical. Victorian glass, which it has been fashionable to denigrate, is being reassessed, and the work of many neglected designers and studios is now receiving the appreciation which it deserves.

A revival of interest in the Midde Ages had begun in the late eighteenth century, when collectors such as Horace Walpole imported from Europe the panels made by medieval craftsmen which can still be seen in his Gothic villa at Strawberry Hill, Twickenham. From handling such pieces, many more of which were imported in the early nineteenth century, glaziers and artists again learned the techniques and styles of medieval glass, and the need to restore, conserve and re-install medieval church glass led to a more archaeologically accurate approach to its study. Influential figures were Charles Winston, who wrote extensively and practically on medieval windows, and who was responsible for great improvements in the quality of glass available through the production of pot-metal in the original colours from 1850, and A. W. N. Pugin (1812-52), the pioneer of the Gothic Revival movement in architecture and church design. Pugin believed that by the direct imitation of medieval techniques the modern craftsman could achieve the spirituality of the Middle Ages. Examples of Pugin's designs for windows, made by his partner John Hardman, can be seen in the House of Lords and, perhaps their masterpiece, the west window of Ushaw College chapel, Durham (1847).

Another pioneer was Thomas Willement, originally a fine painter of heraldic windows, who then studied medieval glass and was the first to rediscover the proper use of the leads in

design. He became stained glass artist to Queen Victoria and made an extensive series of windows for St George's Chapel, Windsor. The glass of the 1840s and 1850s generally closely imitated that of the Middle Ages, with the fourteenth century regarded as the ideal period.

There was then a phase which involved a more inventive recreation of the medieval canon, in particular by three firms founded in response to the ever-increasing demand for stained glass; their best work was produced in the 1860s and is marked by simple, linear designs and strong colours. These were Clayton & Bell (who made the stunning Last Judgement window at Hanley Castle church,Worcestershire, 1860), Heaton, Butler & Bayne (who made the Te Deum window in All Saints, Clapham Park, London, 1862) and Lavers & Barraud (who made the scenes from Tennyson's *Idylls of the King* for Northampton Town Hall, 1862).

The later work of what were to become very large studios shows less individuality, more painterly detail and muted tones but nonetheless inspired the windows of other firms continuing to work in a Gothic Revival manner. These included that of the prolific C. E. Kempe (founded 1869), whose fifteenth-century style can be seen in his many windows, such as those at West Kirby (Merseyside) and Wakefield Cathedral, and of Burlison & Grylls (1868), who produced fine windows such as those for E. F. Bodley's churches at Pendlebury (Lancashire), and Hoar Cross (Staffordshire). These firms all had distinctive and re-cognisable house styles, based on the work of the chief designer for the firm.

James Powell & Sons (subsequently Whitefriars) (1834) took another approach: they employed a series of distinguished freelance artists to design the windows, which Powells made from their own high-quality glass based on the research of Charles Winston; they manufactured his formula for pot-metal. Their style, therefore, ranges from the medievalising Tree of Jesse window (1861) designed by Edward Burne-Jones (then their chief designer) for Waltham Abbey (Essex) to the more aesthetic work of the 1870s and 1880s, designed by artists such

49. (Opposite page) St Martin, Worcester. Transfiguration by Frederick Preedy, 1857, in a loosely fourteenth-century style by an early Gothic Revival designer and architect.

50. (Left) Ely Cathedral: south chancel. Christ walking on the Sea of Galilee by Clayton & Bell, 1860. This early window shows the strong outline and clear colour tones associated with this studio.

51. (Below) Prickwillow, Cambridgeshire: east window. Crucifixion by Heaton, Butler & Bayne, 1860, using the distinctively coloured glass which the firm had especially commissioned.

52. (Right) St Mary, Godmanchester, Cambridgeshire. Detail of the Jesse window by Charles Kempe, 1880; a Victorian use of a medieval subject, showing Kempe's distinctive dark green and silvery palette.

53. (Below) Youlgreave, Derbyshire. Salvator Mundi with the Four Evangelists, 1870s, designed by Edward Burne-Jones and made by Morris & Co.

as William de Morgan (Rocester, Staffordshire), John Hungerford Pollen (Ripon, North Yorkshire) and J. W. Brown (Stillingfleet, North Yorkshire).

A deliberate and rapid reaction against both the style and the mass-production methods of Gothic Revival glass appears in the work produced by the firm founded in 1861 as Morris, Marshall, Faulkner & Co (later to become Morris & Co), established by William Morris with his friends and fellow-artists of the Pre-Raphaelite movement, Peter Paul Marshall, C. J. Faulkner, Dante Gabriel Rossetti, Ford Madox Brown and Burne-Jones (later to become the chief designer). Their windows used new colour tones, including much white glass and a vivid ruby-gold; they replaced the conventional architectural backgrounds by blue and green foliage patterns, and the dominating single figures were designed to relate to the architectural setting. Typically excellent series can be seen at Oxford, in Christ Church Cathedral (1870s) and Manchester College (1890s), and at Cambridge, in Jesus College chapel (1870s). Of their later work, the windows of Birmingham Anglican Cathedral are outstanding. Among other designers initially influenced by the Pre-Raphaelite movement, the most original was Henry Holiday, who first designed for Powells, then founded his own studio. Mortlake church has a beautiful Annunciation in his early style, while his later, more classical manner can be seen in the Creation window of Southwark Cathedral.

Towards the end of the century there was a further reaction against the factory-like processes of so many Victorian studios. A new generation of Arts and Crafts movement workers, emerging from about 1890, demanded that a designer should remain involved throughout the making of a product; in the case of a window the designer should also be responsible for all stages of its execution. Led by Christopher Whall, a group of colleagues and pupils produced windows which had a new emphasis on the transmission of light through the use of the new *slab glass*, whose rich texture was quite unsuitable for the detailed painting techniques of so much Victorian glass. Good examples by Whall himself are at Burford (Oxfordshire) and Gloucester Cathedral.

54 (Opposite page) Ely Cathedral: Stained Glass Museum. Agony in the Garden of Gethsemane by Heaton, Butler & Bayne, 1866, formerly in St Andrew, Bridport, Dorset.

Some innovative windows were also being produced in Scotland by the end of the century, with Glasgow as a focal point. The studio run by the Guthrie brothers employed as freelance designers distinguished artists such as Harrington Mann and David Gauld. Another influential designer was Daniel Cottier, who moved from Glasgow to London, became a prominent member of the Aesthetic movement and subsequently opened studios in New York and Sydney. C. R. Mackintosh was a modernist designer of international reputation who totally integrated glass into his buildings and furnishings.

By the turn of the century, British stained glass held a leading position in the world and was extensively exported. As well as the large-scale and official commissions, many windows were made for domestic settings; glazed and decorated front doors and internal panels were to be fashionable from Victorian times down to the 1930s.

55. (Opposite page) Chelmsford Cathedral: south-west aisle. The Holderness window by Henry Holiday, 1890s.

56. (Right) St Osmund, Ashbourne, Derbyshire. Christopher Whall's portrayal of St Dorothea, 1905.

The twentieth century

By the outbreak of the First World War the Arts and Crafts movement was losing its impetus despite the premises established at the Glass House, Fulham, by Lowndes and Drury as a studio where artists could work independently of the large commercial firms. An ultimately Gothic Revival style was carried on through the work of Sir Ninian Comper, F. C. Eden and the brothers Christopher and Geoffrey Webb. Their detailed figures were often set against clear backgrounds; while the drawing is refined the general effect is sometimes insipid. Much less compromising was the approach of a group of Irish designers, working in the first half of the century, who had benefited from the Dublin studio, the Tower of Glass, founded with Christopher Whall's support. Evie Hone made powerful – almost overpowering – east windows for Eton College chapel (1952) and St Michael, Haringey (London), and her reputation has overshadowed that of Wilhelmina Geddes, whose early work, such as the Crucifixion east window of St Luke, Wallsend-on-Tyne (1922), bears comparison with anything of its time. In contrast to their monumental approach, the glass of Harry Clarke is famous for its intricate detail and vivid colours, as in his windows at Nantwich (Cheshire) and Sturminster Newton (Dorset) (1921). In Scotland also, the Arts and Crafts tradition was maintained by several designers, including Louis Davis, William Wilson and Douglas Strachan (Edinburgh Castle chapel).

Another distinctive designer was the Hungarian painter Ervin Bossanyi (1891-1975), whose very personal and figurative style can be seen at Canterbury Cathedral and York Minster. Rather less figurative were the first windows designed by John Piper and made in collaboration with Patrick Reyntiens, for Oundle School chapel, Northamptonshire, in 1955. These were a milestone in modern English glass, marking the beginning of a long and distinguished partnership, some of whose other works can be seen at Eton College (1959-64)) and Robinson College chapel, Cambridge (1979), as well as the baptistry window of Coventry Cathedral (1962).

The commissions for Coventry represented a resurgence in English stained glass in the scale involved and the use of abstract design; the nave windows were made by a collaborative team from the Royal College of Art, Lawrence Lee, Keith New and Geoffrey Clarke, who have all done important work elsewhere. As an integral part of its construction the Roman

57. Southwark Cathedral, London: Harvard Chapel. Window by the American John La Farge (1836-1906), who, like his friend and rival Tiffany, experimented with new glass techniques.

Catholic cathedral at Liverpool (1965-7) has abstract glass designed by Piper and Reyntiens, Margaret Traherne and Ceri Richards. This is in total contrast to the glass of the Anglican cathedral at Liverpool, which has the more figural styles of the earlier part of the century, made by Whitefriars; the great west window was designed in 1979 by Carl Edwards.

Other striking examples of modern glass can be seen in Salisbury Cathedral, in the 'Prisoners of Conscience' window (1980) by Gabriel Loire, a glazier from Chartres, whose work in *dalle de verre* is also installed in the chapel at Strawberry Hill, Twickenham, and St Richard, Chichester. In Chichester Cathedral is a series of windows made from the vivid but delicate figural designs of Marc Chagall; another set, in characteristic blue tones, is at Tudeley, Kent. A younger generation of British designers, including Alan Younger, Brian Clarke, Amber Hiscott and Mark Angus, are producing major abstract works for secular buildings as well as for churches: there is an increasing number of windows in offices, pubs, hotels and shopping centres.

The conflict between the abstract and the more figural traditions of glass is also that between modern and traditional architecture. For stained glass to have a healthy future, which

58. St Peter and St Paul, Aldeburgh, Suffolk: north aisle. Benjamin Britten memorial window by John Piper and Patrick Reyntiens (1979) depicting Britten's three operas, *The Prodigal Son*, *Curlew River* and *The Burning Fiery Furnace*.

59. (Above left) Sheffield Cathedral: Chapel of the Holy Spirit. Te Deum by Christopher Webb.

60. (Above right) Derby Cathedral: south aisle, east window. All Saints designed by Ceri Richards and made by Patrick Reyntiens; it is paired by All Souls in the north aisle.

61. (Below) St Albert, Stockbridge, Liverpool. The Annunciation by Alf Fisher and Peter Archer, 1976, modern designers using the symbols of the Virgin – the lily and the dove.

can reflect its glorious past, it is essential that more patronage is forthcoming from the secular field, with designs relating to the needs of contemporary buildings. Although the autonomous or free-standing panel has become a popular mode of expression in stained glass and is sold in galleries in the same way as a painting, stained glass must also remain an integral element of the architecture of the future; it is this which will ensure the continuing development of this exciting medium.

Identifying windows

Some windows are signed and dated or marked by the emblems of their makers; these are normally very small and are often placed in one of the lower margins. Such marks were extremely rare in medieval times but became more frequent in the nineteenth and twentieth centuries. They can be based upon monograms or puns on the name of the artist or studio.

Many windows have inscriptions with the date of death of the person being commemorated; this does not necessarily mean that the window was made in that year, but only that it could not have been made before that date. However it is a useful way of giving an approximate date to the many nineteenth-century windows which are otherwise unrecorded.

Thomas
Willement

Charles E.
Kempe

Powell & Sons
of Whitefriars

M. Farrer Bell

62. The four marks above represent many which have been identified in recent years, particularly by the Church Recorders of the National Association of Decorative and Fine Arts Societies. Their information on glaziers of the nineteenth and twentieth centuries is published in *Stained Glass Makers' Marks*.

5
Places to visit

The list is a necessarily brief selection of the buildings in Britain containing interesting or important stained glass. In the majority of places named below the windows are in the local parish church. The numbers in the list refer to centuries. For example, at Bath Abbey there is good stained glass of the seventeenth, nineteenth and twentieth centuries.

ENGLAND

Avon Bath: Abbey 17, 19, 20; St Bartholomew 20. Bristol: All Saints 20; Cathedral 14, 15, 19, 20; St Mary Redcliffe 15, 19, 20. Brockley 19. Winscombe 15, 16.

Bedfordshire Cockayne Hatley 14, 15, 18. Edworth 14. Luton: St Mary 15, 20. Northill 17. Totternhoe 20.

Berkshire Aldermaston 13. Bradfield College 19. Bucklebury 17. Eton College chapel 20. Ockwells Manor 15. Slough: St Mary 19, 20. Stratfield Mortimer 15, 19. Windsor: St George 19, 20.

Buckinghamshire Bradenham 16, 18. Chetwode 13, 14. Drayton Beauchamp 15. Frieth 19. Hillesden 16. Marlow 20. Monks Risborough 15. Stoke Poges 17, 19. Turville 16, 18. Weston Underwood 14.

Cambridgeshire Buckden 15. Cambridge: All Saints 19, 20; Jesus College 19; King's College 16; Peterhouse 17, 19; Robinson College 20; St John's College 19; Trinity College 18. Diddington 15, 16, 17. Ely Cathedral 14, 19, 20. Haslingfield 14. Kimbolton 20. Leverington 15. Meldreth 14, 19. Peterborough Cathedral 19. Sawtry 15, 16. Thorney 15, 19. Trumpington 13. Wistow 15.

Cheshire Chester Cathedral 19. Crewe 20. Daresbury 20. Disley 16. Grappenhall 16. Marple 19, 20. Nantwich 19, 20. Shotwick 14.

Cornwall Cotehele House 16. Ladock 19. St Kew 15. St Neot 15, 16. St Winnow 15, 16. Truro Cathedral 19.

Cumbria Ambleside 19. Bowness 14, 15. Brampton 19. Cartmel Fell 14, 15. Greystoke 16. Keswick 19, 20. Lanercost 19, 20. Tolson Hall 17. Troutbeck 19. Windermere: St John Evangelist 20.

Derbyshire Ashbourne 13, 14, 15, 19, 20. Dalbury 11. Darley Dale 19. Derby Cathedral 20. Dronfield 14. Morley 15. Norbury 14, 15, 20. Staveley 14, 17, 20. Swanwick 20. Wilne 17.

Devon Ashton 15. Bampton 15. Bere Ferrers 14. Broadwood Kelly 16. Doddiscombsleigh 15, 19, 20. Exeter Cathedral 14, 15, 18, 19, 20. Ilfracombe 19. Ottery St Mary 19. Plymouth: St Andrew 20. Tavistock 19. Torquay: St John 19.

Dorset Abbotsbury 14, 18. Bournemouth: St Peter 19. Bradford Peverell 15. Cattistock 19, 20. Melbury Bubb 15. Sherborne Abbey 19. Sturminster Newton 19, 20.

Durham Durham: Cathedral 14, 15, 19, 20; St Oswald 19. Lanchester 13. Raby Castle 12, 13. Ushaw: St Cuthbert's College 19.

Essex Audley End 18. Basildon: St Martin 20. Clavering 15. Great Burstead 15. Harlow: St Mary 14, 18, 19. Heybridge 13. Margaretting 15. Messing 17. Prittlewell 16, 19, 20. Rivenhall 12, 13. Stapleford Abbotts 14. Thaxted 14, 15. Waltham Abbey 19, 20.

Gloucestershire Arlingham 14, 15. Bagendon 15, 20. Bibury 13, 19, 20. Bledington 15. Buckland 15. Cheltenham: St Mary 19. Cirencester 15. Coln Rogers 15. Deerhurst 14. Fairford 16. Gloucester Cathedral 14, 19, 20. North Cerney 15, 20. Prinknash 20. Selsley 19. Temple Guiting 15. Tewkesbury Abbey 14, 19.

Hampshire Bramley 14, 16. East Tytherley 13, 14. Grateley 13. Headley 13. Herriard 14. Hinton Ampner 20. Lyndhurst 19. Mottisfont 15. Sherborne St John: the Vyne 16, 18. Winchester: Cathedral 15, 16, 19, 20; College chapel 14, 19; St Cross Hospital 15, 19.

Herefordshire Abbey Dore 15, 16, 17. Brinsop 14, 20. Brockhampton 20. Credenhill 14. Eaton Bishop 14. Hereford Cathedral 14, 19, 20. Ledbury 13, 16, 19, 20. Madley 13, 14. Ross-on-Wye: St Mary 15. Sellack 15, 16, 17. Weobley 15.

Hertfordshire Barkway 14, 15. Barley 14, 15, 16. Cuffley 20. Gorhambury House 16, 17. Hatfield House 17. High Cross 19. King's Walden 19. St Albans Cathedral 19, 20. St Paul's Walden 14, 20. South Mimms 16. Waterford 19, 20.

Humberside Barton-upon-Humber 14. Beverley Minster 13, 14, 15, 19. Harpham 18. Hotham 20. Redbourne 18. South Dalton 19.

Isle of Wight Bonchurch 19.

Kent Boughton Aluph 14. Brabourne 12, 15. Canterbury Cathedral 12, 13, 15, 20. Chartham 13. Chilham 15. Cobham 20. Doddington 13. Fawkham 14. Farningham 19, 20. Nackington 13. Nettlestead 15. Penshurst 19, 20. Selling 14. Tonbridge School 20. Tudeley 20. Upper Hardres 13, 14. Westwell 13, 14. Wickhambreux 19.

Lancashire Ashton-under-Lyne 15, 16. Blackburn Cathedral 19,

20. Easby 20. Habergham 20. Leyland 20. Longridge 20. Lytham 19. Manchester: Cathedral 20; St Anne 18, 19. Middleton 16, 20. Tunstall 15, 16.

Leicestershire Appleby 14. Ayston 15. Hallaton 19. Leicester: Cathedral 20; Museum 15, 16. North Luffenham 14, 19. Preston 19, 20. Thornton 14. Twycross 12, 13. Whitwell 14. Withcote 16.

Lincolnshire Carlton Scroop 14. Grantham 19, 20. Heydour 14. Lincoln Cathedral 12, 13, 14, 18, 19, 20. Long Sutton 14. Raithby-by-Louth 19. Stamford: Browne's Hospital 15; St George 15; St Martin 15, 16, 19. Stragglethorpe 13. Tattershall 15. Wrangle 14.

London (Greater) Bromley: St Mary 20. City of London: St Andrew Undershaft 17; St Botolph, Aldersgate 18, 19, 20. City of Westminster: All Saints, Margaret Street 15, 19; St George, Hanover Square 16; St Margaret, Westminster, 16, 19, 20; Westminster Abbey 13, 15, 18, 19, 20. Greenwich: Trinity Hospital 16. Haringey: St Michael 20. Havering: Hornchurch 20. Kensington and Chelsea: Sloane Street, Holy Trinity 19; Victoria and Albert Museum, all periods. Lambeth: Palace 16, 19, 20; St Mary 19, 20. Merton: St Mary, Wimbledon 14, 17, 20. Richmond-upon-Thames: St Mary's College, Strawberry Hill, Twickenham 16, 17, 20. Southwark: Cathedral 19, 20. Wandsworth: All Saints 19.

Merseyside Allerton 19. Liverpool: Anglican Cathedral 20; RC Cathedral 20. Port Sunlight 20. West Kirby 19.

Norfolk Aylsham 19. Bawburgh 14, 15. East Harling 15. Elsing 14. Erpingham 15, 16. Ketteringham 15. Langley 15, 16, 19. Martham 15, 19. Mulbarton 16, 19. North Elmham 14. North Tuddenham 15. Norwich: Cathedral 16, 19, 20; Guildhall 15; St John Baptist 19; St Peter Hungate 15, 16; St Peter Mancroft 15, 20. Saxlingham Nethergate 13, 14, 15, 19, 20. Sculthorpe 19. Shelton 15, 16. South Acre 13. Stratton Strawless 15. Thurton 15, 17, 19.

Northamptonshire Aldwincle 14. Apethorpe 17, 18. Hollowell 19. Lowick 14. Mears Ashby 19, 20. Middleton Cheney 19. Oundle School chapel 20. Rushden 15. Stanford-on-Avon 14, 15, 16, 19. Watford 19. Wellingborough: All Saints 19, 20.

Northumberland Alnwick 19. Bothal 14, 15. Morpeth 14.

Nottinghamshire Babworth 18, 19. Bleasby 20. Hawton 14. Holme-by-Newark 15. Hucknall 20. Keyworth 20. Misterton 20. Newark 14, 15, 19. Southwell Minster 14, 16, 17, 19.

Oxfordshire Bloxham 19. Burford 15, 19, 20. Childrey 15. Chinnor 14, 19, 20. Dorchester Abbey 13, 14, 19. Harpsden 15. Horspath 13, 14, 15, 16. Kidlington 13, 15, 19. Marsh Baldon 14, 15. Nettlebed 20. Oxford: All Souls College 15, 19; Balliol

College 16, 17, 19; Brasenose College 18, 19; Christ Church Cathedral 14, 17, 19; Exeter College 19; Lincoln College 17; Merton College 13, 15, 16; New College 14, 18; Nuffield College 20; Queen's College 16, 17, 18; Trinity College 14, 15, 16, 17, 19; University College 17, 19. South Newington 14. Stanford-in-the-Vale 14. Stanton Harcourt 13, 15. Stanton St John 13, 14. Wroxton Abbey 17. Yarnton 15, 16, 17.

Shropshire Atcham 15. Cressage 19. Donnington 14. Ludlow: St Laurence 14, 15, 19, 20. Meole Brace 19. Prees 19. Shrewsbury: St Mary 14, 15, 16, 17, 19. Upton Magna 19.

Somerset Axbridge Town Hall 15. Compton Bishop 14. Glaston-bury 19, 20. Langport 15, 19. Low Ham 17. Wells Cathedral 14, 15, 17, 18, 19, 20.

Staffordshire Amington 19. Cheddleton 19. Hamstall Ridware 13, 14, 16, 19. Leigh 14, 19. Lichfield Cathedral 16, 19. Okeover 14, 19. Tamworth 19, 20. Trysull 14, 19.

Suffolk Aldeburgh 20. Barton Mills 14. Brandeston 16. Brandon 19. Bury St Edmunds Cathedral 16, 19. Combs 14, 15. Gipping 15. Hengrave Hall 16. Herringswell 20. Hessett 15. Ipswich: St Mary le Tower 19. Long Melford 15. Lowestoft: St Margaret 15, 19, 20; St Matthew 19. Snape 20. Thorndon 14, 15.

Surrey Ashtead 16. Buckland 14, 15. Chiddingfold 14, 15. Compton 13, 17. Guildford: Abbot's Hospital 17; Cathedral 20. Hindhead 20. Laleham 20. Stoke D'Abernon 15, 16, 17. Sutton Place 16, 17, 19. West Horsley 13.

Sussex, East and West Arundel 19. Bexhill: St Peter 15. Brighton: St Michael 19. Chichester: Cathedral 19, 20; St Richard 20. Eastbourne 20. Lancing College 19. Loxwood 20. Ovingdean 19. Northchapel 20. Rottingdean 19. Ticehurst 14. Winchelsea 14, 20.

Tyne and Wear Jarrow Museum 8. Newcastle upon Tyne: Cathedral 15, 19, 20; St John Baptist 15. Sunderland: Christchurch 19. Wallsend 20.

Warwickshire Arley 14. Cherington 14, 15, 16. Coughton 16. Mancetter 14. Merevale 14, 15. Warwick: St Mary 15, 19, 20. Willoughby 20. Wroxall Abbey 14.

West Midlands Aston 18. Binley 18. Birmingham: Cathedral 19; St Paul 18. Cheylesmore 20. Coventry: Cathedral 15, 20; St Mary's Hall 15, 20. Dudley: St Thomas 19. Wightwick Manor 19. Wolverhampton 20.

Wiltshire Cricklade 19, 20. Crudwell 15. Edington 15. Lydiard Tregoze 15, 17. Mere 14, 19. Salisbury Cathedral 13, 14, 17, 18, 19, 20. Stourhead 15. Wilton 12, 13, 14, 15, 16, 17.

Worcestershire Bredon 14. Fladbury 14, 19. Great Malvern Priory 15, 19. Great Witley 18. Hanley Castle 19. Holt 15. Kempsey 14. Little Malvern 15. Mamble 14. Oddingley 16. Warndon 14, 15. Worcester Cathedral 19.

Yorkshire, North Coxwold 15, 18. Denton-in-Wharfedale 17. Gilling Castle 16. Knaresborough 19. Scarborough 19. Selby Abbey 14, 19. Tadcaster 14, 15, 19, 20. York: All Saints 14, 15; Holy Trinity, Goodramgate 15; Minster 13, 14, 15, 16, 17, 18, 19, 20; St Denys, Walmgate 14, 15; St Helen 14, 15; St Martin 15; St Michael, Spurriergate 15, 16. **Yorkshire, South** Doncaster: St George 19. Sheffield Cathedral 19, 20. **Yorkshire, West** Adel 17. Almondbury 15. Bradford Cathedral 19, 20. Ilkley 19, 20. Normanton 13, 14, 15, 16, 17. Rothwell 18, 19. Thornhill 15, 18.

SCOTLAND

Central Dunblane Cathedral 20.

Fife Culross Abbey 20. Dunfermline Abbey 20. Kirkcaldy: St Brycedale 19, 20. St Andrews: Holy Trinity 19, 20. Upper Largo 19, 20.

Grampian Aberdeen: King's College chapel 19, 20. Crathie 19. Fyvie 20.

Lothian Edinburgh: Café Royal 19; Castle chapel 20; St Giles Cathedral 19, 20; St Cuthbert, Lothian Road 19, 20. Linlithgow: St Michael 19, 20. Roslin Chapel 20.

Strathclyde Douglas 13. Glasgow Cathedral 16, 17, 19, 20. Greenock: West Kirk 19. Largs: Clark Memorial Church 19. Paisley Abbey 19, 20. Pollokshields 19, 20.

Tayside Brechin Cathedral 19, 20. Perth: St John 19, 20.

WALES

Clwyd Dyserth 16. Gresford 15, 18, 19. Hawarden 19, 20. Llanasa 16, 19. Llandyrnog 16. Llangollen: Plas Newydd 15, 16, 17, 18; St Collen 19. Llanrhaedr 15, 16. Tremeirchion 16, 17. Treuddyn 14.

Dyfed Cardigan: Our Lady 20. Fishguard 20. Lampeter 19, 20. Newport 14, 17, 19, 20. Pembroke Dock 19, 20. St Davids Cathedral 15, 19, 20. Spittal 20. Tenby: St Mary 19, 20.

Glamorgan Bridgend Crematorium 20. Llandaff Cathedral 19, 20. Porthcawl 20. Swansea: St David 15, 20; St Mary 20.

Gwent Newport: St Woolos Cathedral 20.

Gwynedd Holyhead 19, 20. Llanuwchllyn 15, 16. Penrhyn Castle 19.

Powys Llangattock 19. Llyswen 20. Old Radnor 15. Welshpool 19.

6
Museums with general collections of stained glass

Birmingham Museum and Art Gallery, Chamberlain Square, Birmingham B3 3DH. Telephone: 0121-235 2834.

Bradford Art Gallery, Cartwright Hall, Lister Park, Bradford BD9 4NS. Telephone: 01274 493313.

Burrell Collection, 2060 Pollokshaws Road, Glasgow G43 1AT. Telephone: 0141-649 7151.

Pilkington Glass Museum, Prescot Road, St Helens, Merseyside WA10 3TT. Telephone: 01744 692499.

The Stained Glass Museum, North Triforium, The Cathedral, Ely, Cambridgeshire CB7 4DN. Telephone: 01353 667735, extension 247.

Victoria and Albert Museum, Cromwell Road, South Kensington, London SW7 2RL. Telephone: 0171-938 8500.

Winchester City Museum, The Square, Winchester, Hampshire SO23 9ES. Telephone: 01962 848269.

7
Further reading

Angus, M. *Modern Stained Glass in British Churches.* Mowbray, 1984.

Brisac, C. *A Thousand Years of Stained Glass.* MacDonald, 1986.

Brown, S. *An Illustrated History of Stained Glass.* Studio, 1992.

Brown, S., and O'Connor, D. *Glass Painters.* British Museum, 1991.

Cowen, P. *A Guide to Stained Glass in Britain.* Michael Joseph, 1985.

Cowen, P. *Rose Windows.* Thames & Hudson, 1984.

Crewe, S. *Stained Glass in England 1180-1540.* HMSO, 1987.

Harrison, M. *Victorian Stained Glass.* Barrie & Jenkins, 1980.

Morris, E. *Stained and Decorative Glass.* Tiger Books International, 1990.

Osborne, J. *Stained Glass in England.* Alan Sutton, 1993.

Reyntiens, P. *The Beauty of Stained Glass.* Herbert Press, 1990.

Stained Glass Makers' Marks. Available from the National Association of Decorative and Fine Arts Societies (NADFAS), 8 Guilford Street, London WC1 1DT.

Index

Page numbers in italic refer to illustrations.